STRANGE BEAUTY SHOWS

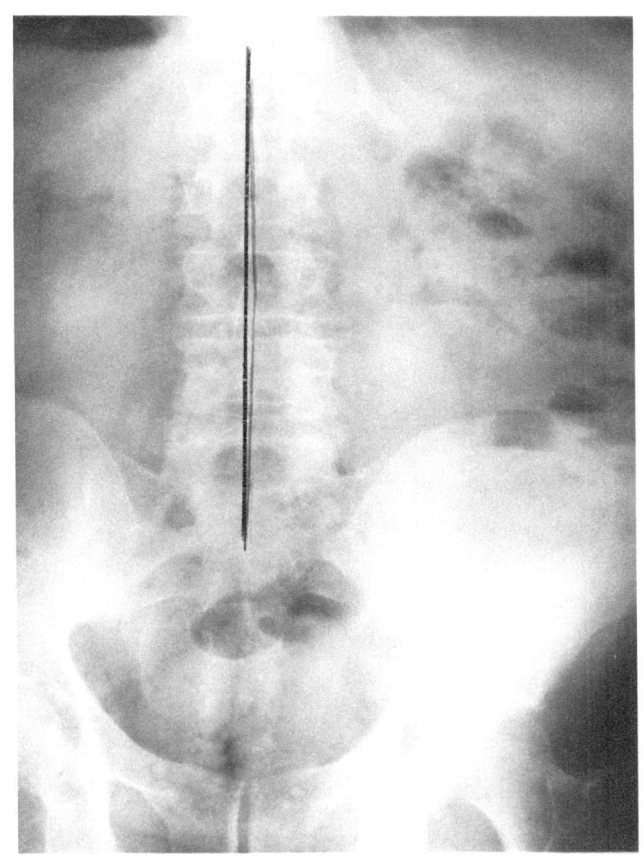

Poems by Steven H. Bridgens

Kansas City　　　Missouri

Spartan Press
Kansas City, Missouri
spartanpresskc.com

Copyright (c) 2017 Steven H. Bridgens
First Edition 1 3 5 7 9 10 8 6 4 2
ISBN: 978-1-946642-10-3
LCCN: 2017931603

Design and layout: Jason Ryberg
Edits: Jason Ryberg, Will Leathem, Tom Wayne,
Author photo: David Haggard, Sonia Spotts
X-rays: Front cover and title page: Dr. Meagan Leahy, D.C.,
Back cover: Dickson Diveley Orthopedic Clinic PA
All rights reserved. No part of this publication may be reproduced or transmitted in any form or by any means, electronic or mechanical, including photocopying, recording or by info retrieval system, without prior written permission from the author.

ACKNOWLEDGMENTS

Prospero's Books and Spartan Press would like to thank Jeanette Powers, j.d.tulloch, Jason Preu, M. Scott Douglass, Shawn Pavey, Shaun Savings, Jesse Kates, Jim Holroyd, Steven H. Bridgens, Thomas Mason, Beth Dille, Mason Wolf, The West Plaza Tomato Co., The Osage Arts Community and The Robert J. Deuser Foundation For Libertarian Studies.

The author would like to thank: Sue Adair, Jon Bidwell, Kate Ghio, Patricia Grey, David Haggard, Tanya Kelley, Will Leathem, Patricia Cleary Miller, Betty Mantz, Geoff Oelsner, Jane Pearce, Lazarus Potter, Andrés Rodríguez, Jason Ryberg, Nancy Seelan, Sonia Spotts, Kathy Ann Tate, Tom Wayne, Rick Zander.

CONTENTS

The Titanic Lookout / 1

Ask a Guy / 2

I'm Really No One / 3

The River Waits / 4

A Leviathan, I Glimpsed / 5

Poetry / 6

Right a Poem / 8

Professional Courtesy / 9

Days Full of Surprises / 10

Skeletal Beauty Here / 12

The Decorator's Lament / 13

So When? / 14

Eloquent Silence / 15

Moon Tea at Midnight / 16

Some Wet Science / 17

Manifested Across Town / 18

All Now Sunk and Long Ago Gone / 19

Sink or Swim / 20

The Lonely Radio / 21

The Moth and the Flame / 22

Discussing the Storm / 23

Joining the Mermaids / 24

A Crack Only / 25

Leaving Poems on the Floor / 26

In the Old Neighborhood / 27

To the Blond Tara / 28

These Leaves / 30

The Monkey Lab / 31

Wireless Out Here / 32

Slow Boats and Magic Mountains / 33

Swept Away / 34

Out on the Land / 35

That's the Thing / 36

No Trains / 37

Minor Napoleonia / 38

The Miracle of Leverage / 39

On A Beautiful Day Like This / 40

Strange Magic Incarnate / 41

Loud and Clear / 42

I Live Alone Now / 43

Rural Drama / 44

The *Ticks* of the *Tock* / 46

Crickets in Fall / 48

Most Young Men / 49

the seconds / 50

An Anarchist Miracle / 51

A Poem, Hopefully / 52

We Never Auditioned / 53

Every Man Dreaming of Crime / 54

At Three Gorges with Li Po / 55

One Breath / 56

Twin Bed / 57

Here Again / 58
The Princess and the Peacock / 59
Darn That Dream! / 60
The Great Peregrination / 61
Dawn Breaks / 62
A Bird's Careful Life / 63
Fine Horseflesh / 64
The National Pastime / 65
So Sorry, Old Chap / 66
SPDRS and ZEBRAS / 67
Another Bud / 68
A Word to the Wise Guy / 69
That Final Cool Somewhere / 70
When My Time / 71
A Treatise in a Smile / 72
The Poem's Cooked / 73
May Already / 74
what is called a hill / 75
After Dinner Remarks / 76
A Father's Job, That / 78
bask in the light / 79
The Voices, All Mine / 80
My Plaster Sky / 81
the laughing musical stream of life / 82
Cicadas Interrupted / 85
This Yeller Light / 87

To my son, Arthur and my brother, R. Getty
and in the deepest background
Virginia Scott Miner

To all of my muses, every one

His empty eyes stare at strange beauty shows

- Mick Jagger and Keith Richards
Salt of the Earth, Beggar's Banquet

The Titanic Lookout

You asked me once what I thought.
But like the lookout on the Titanic,
I can only report what I thought I saw.

What's left unseen and unsaid,
even I cannot fully fathom.

I told you the truth, what I knew of it then
and lately I've been intensifying my search.

These humble missives are the result.

Ask A Guy

Ask a guy who knows. It's not in books or parking lots.
It's on lonely beaches where ageless particles
are crushed by eternal waves.

It lays down on everything like lead-based paint
but with that certain lambent fire,
amazing to the eyes when it's finally turned on.

These are dedicated to you, who've led me to so many
wondrous and dangerous places in myself,
through no fault of your own.

May you continue to amuse, be it near or be it far.

I'm Really No One

I'm really no one, passing through this airport of souls.

I'm nobody special, just a fuckin' genius
like everyone else.

Go ahead, hand me a shovel and I'll show you
how it's done.

I hope you get the right tool for your job.

It's hell trying to change an engine with chopsticks.

The River Waits

There was, finally, no need for me
to keep making such a fool of myself,
swilling bottomless buckets of *spirtus fermenti,*
anxiously awaiting brief moonlit visits from my muse.

I no longer need to look under the bed
to see who (or what) lurks there, patiently waiting.
Now, instead of insanely screaming
at my neighbor's howling dogs, I sit quietly,
calmly oiling my Luger in the dark.

I still carry a swollen briefcase of pretense packed tightly
with my cross, my millstone and my albatross.
I just want to be another well-dressed guy,
a member of the team, pulling his weight,
waking Monday morning, *daisy fresh,*
once again believing in the promise of America.

But alas, there is always a skull in the lap of luxury,
the Illuminati still runs the show, the cats are in their sack
and the moody river waits.

A Leviathan, I Glimpsed

The glory of it, rising up like that,
the dark sea parted momentarily,
a leviathan, I glimpsed,
a veritable Jeroboam of a poem,
a giant pterodactyl it was,
flying into the sun—gone.

No fucking pencil.

Poetry

It is small, tiny, puissant, unctuous. It fits in your pocket
with room to spare, between your car keys and dad's beat-up
pocket knife. It will pass through security, but just barely.

Poetry sees around corners in the best and worst
neighborhoods and in any kind of weather.
Frogs and toads have been shown to like it, that is to say,
they respond positively in experimental settings.

Poetry reveals itself in stages. It's coy, like Andrew Marvell's
mistress. It should be, shouldn't it, because what's the fun
of getting it all on the first date?

It does take a lot of hard rubbing, however,
to bring out that tumescent, ruddy glow. I said it was tiny,
like the cramped spaces between the memes.
Audio dust can gather there if care is not taken.

In any case, it should be pointed out that regardless
of the size of the poem, the wind blows harder as you
near the summit. Retaining a firm grip and a deft touch
is highly recommended, always, as in most undertakings.

The rules are many, the exceptions few. Apply both
at your peril. Advice and direction in refining one's craft
is fine and dandy and horrible in one short meeting.

Finally, it is thin beer on a cold winter's night
before a roaring fire with your manuscript in hand,
tattered and torn, and the hearth demons living in the flames
singing out every which way—*Here, let us look.*

Once you start down the slippery slope of poetry,
be careful not to eat anything along the way,
perhaps just a few pomegranate seeds,
to take the edge off your hunger.
Scheduling issues will certainly ensue.

My long dead therapist (sadly lost after a sudden
unscheduled meeting between a divine red Alfa Romeo
and a stubborn telephone pole), called it a sublime
replacement therapy, merely exchanging one
crippling addiction for another.

Forget about the bread crumbs,
they just make a mess and the poems crummy.
It's easy to piss away happy and tragic hours
in pursuit of poetry but hey, what do you think
you would be doing otherwise?

Then let me tell you this, it won't make a spitball's worth
of difference, one way or another.

Right a Poem

I'm going to right a poem, just pull it out of my guts.
I'll feel it forever like your smile, your tears
that have fallen on to my raggedy sleeve.

You have graced me with your presence,
a tiny bit of your sweet life touching mine.

You pull so sadly, so sweetly at my heart strings,
the joy wells up in me like a geyser, like smoke,
like a flowering pillar of rock and ice, a mountain.

I want to join you, to melt with you into the dream
that ends all things but still, I won't be your grindstone,
feather or crossing guard.

Professional Courtesy
for my father, James Getty Bridgens, M.D.

We all walk the scalpel's edge every day, don't we?
The sharp end of life, always now, now, now.
It's the only time we have.

History, conjecture, fabled stories,
rumors of our glorious past
and the dreams of our utopian science fiction future,
all phantom delusion.

Mother still casts a long shadow across my life,
but, remarkably, Father does, too. He toppled early.
His heart exploded (literally), finally unable to hold back
that vast cornucopia of emotion.

He pulled his own plug, a professional courtesy to us all.

We miss him, of course, but not now.

Days Full of Surprises

Do you feel the pressure of your days adding up?
The leaky boat, the seasick bag, the roaring falls ahead
as you sail merrily, merrily on downstream?

Have you caught a glimpse of your chums in the distance
as they struggle to hold onto their boats
only to finally drop off into memory?

The days and nights flash by us like lighthouse beacons.
Friends don't call. They can't keep up either,
just too busy worrying about their own time warp
and the colostomy bag of death that awaits us all.

I just want to gingerly grasp a few brief moments of joy,
gaiety and plunder before I pull the heavy wooden lid
down over my head on the way to that final, urgent
and unscheduled meeting with *the conqueror worm*.

Eat well, my hearties! I certainly have. The buffet here is
apparently infinite. But I'm still hungry, thirsty, sleepy,
and then, like clockwork, the tides wash me up here
again at the doorsteps of yet another pagan Spring—
still breathing every day, in and out, in and out.

I turn to see flocks of birds heading North one minute,
then turning tail Southward the next, and me, breathless,
as I watch leaves fall, spiders web and fatten, as we all slide
inexorably into our comic holiday darkness.

My heart's beating, usually, but sometimes it's gone
missing, lost in the immense canyon of my chest.
It's such a relief to find it again,
the real source of my meager powers,

and that fatty stuff between my ears remains
a tiny chatterbox of fluff. Though happily,
sometimes from deep inside my sugary protein fog,
a poem pushes itself on through:

> *incalculably amusing, full of surprises,*
> *bedazzled, brilliantly freckled, suntanned,*
> *oily and giggling with an anklet and a*
> *flashing jeweled scimitar.*

Skeletal Beauty Here

Each tiny moment strung together with its brother,
sister and neighbor adds up to lives
measured out in coffee spoons and Kleenex.

One stirs the trouble pot. The other wipes away the tears.

Dragonflies and cicadas flicker and buzz, then are gone,
their skeletal beauty here only an instant.

Are we so different? We can't see our wings.
But they are here all right. They are here.

The Decorator's Lament

I want you in *Empire,* my *Recamier.*
I will wrap you in ermine, my starlet.

I want you on *Biedermeier,* in my palace,
my plaything on a pedestal.
We shall dine on *Directoire*, my suite.

You will be the subject of tomes and tomes,
lyrics upon lyrics for scores of dark fugues.

We'll drink Jeroboam after Jeroboam
while whistling down the caviar.*
My infirmities pass with each silken step.
I play on and on, *sotto voce,* no one listening.

*Noel Coward

So When?

What is that ineffable act of pressing together
our blood-swollen, nerve-filled protuberances?
It's kissing, that almost wholly spiritual act,
the sweet soft flesh being the smallest part of it.

The two, of course, gently touch their lips together
(if for the first time then tentatively, almost,
or actually afraidish), but also unafraid, too

and soon, perhaps, if further emboldened,
if any acceptance (at all) is sensed,
then more warmly and maybe more hopeful
then suddenly hot, miraculously hot,

that passage of breath, warm and wet,
coming up from those two sweet throats
that serve to further ignite, to excite,
to enflame the two, of course, (not coarse)
but fine (mighty fine), one fine day.

So, when does the kissing begin?

Eloquent Silence

Silence is so eloquent.
Your empty high heels walk backwards down my hall.
Your silk kimono gathers dust. I can't wear it anymore.

Every car that passes, I turn expectantly.
I try to fill my days constructively—
a living hell of my own creation.

Moon Tea at Midnight

I don't seem to exert much control over things these days
(as if I ever did), the clock unplugged, to halt time (of course),
dust everywhere (surely I could do more).

The days and nights endlessly flickering away
until my own mysterious, tragic end
(not really much control of that either).

The dawn birds at my window relentlessly sing
to the ambulance racing away in the darkness
towards yet another honking, late night freight.

I turn to listen, and then turn back
to these few tiny words
scratched on this half-empty and futile page,
as my long-dreamed-of lover in her bare feet
makes me moon tea at midnight.

Her mysterious comings and goings,
her humming, quiet smile.

(How could I ever control that?)

Some Wet Science

Words, smiles and tears don't last long but they are often
remembered.

A softly spoken word dissipates too soon after its creation
in a heart and mind, its vibration resonates from deep
within a chest and throat, now here and now gone.

That smile is an exercise of the same mouth and those same lips.
It springs from the same mind that creates, remembers
and then forgets.

Tears, the salty upwelling of our inner sea, created by our own
weather, our own chemistry are pulled up to the inner eye
to then slide effortlessly across that cheek.

They're drawn down mysteriously by some tide, some gravity,
some wet science, to then fall from that tear-tracked cheek,
perhaps onto a sleeve or a hand holding a pencil,
a simple tool for asking.

Manifested Across Town

I've been writing a bit of fiction lately,
trying to paint an imaginary world
with my big brush.

It's fascinating to watch the words
pour out of my purple pen
straight into my notebook here,
on my café table, next to a small black coffee.

You sat in that chair there, then,
and you're disembodied here, now.
And, yes, you're also manifested
somewhere across town, too—no doubt
putting up hay with the stable boy.

We often talked about the sweet bird of paradise,
landing only in the hand that does not grasp,
still perhaps the hardest lesson I have yet to learn.

Sometimes it does pay to throw
your most precious pebble
into that roaring, riotous stream.

All Now Sunk and Long Ago Gone

I started hearing stories about the sea long ago,
about the Phoenicians sailing everywhere, fearlessly,
in their little lateen-rigged ships of olive wood
and Syrian cedar, trading with the lost tribes.

And I heard about Ulysses and his journey home
after that mythic little war. And Aeneas and Jason—
I heard about them. They shipped out, too, leaving
Troy and Carthage in flames behind them.

I heard about Cleo and Tony, the young lovers.
It didn't turn out so well for them at sea, as I recall.
Those crazy kids, thinking they could get one over
on the evil empire.

They almost had it made until she turned tail at Actium.
Then, after sailing home to Alexandria, she took the little
ring'd asp to her breast as her dreams of empire fell apart.
She abandoned Tony to twist endlessly in that dry Egyptian
wind, that still blows in from Homer's wine dark sea.

And, as I said, the big ships with those big guns,
like the thousand that Menelaus sent to Troy after Helen
(that little bitch), are all now sunk, and long ago gone,
like me, forever trapped, burning and drowned,
in your tawny, tiger eyes.

Sink or Swim

It's easy asking a poet to lunch, especially when she
sets the time, place and menu.

I was early, a poor poet without portfolio,
and she was right on time—the food, the talk,
her sea-green eyes, a dream then, just a memory now.

I write these lines on a cardboard scrap,
discovered while walking along the headlands
of these rough, rock-faced dreadnoughts here,
heading eternally South-Southwest into the Pacific wind.

The mussels and barnacles living here are eaten by otters,
sea birds, sous-chefs and the like. They're tough little
critters, clinging to their homes here,
pounded mercilessly by the sea every day.

Poets are like that too, hanging onto whatever is at hand,
an overturned hull, a soul, a mirror, trying only to let go.

The Lonely Radio

The lonely radio in my head plays my poems
and love songs all day long. I know you're out there
somewhere with your radio on, too,
but what songs you play, I haven't a clue.

It's said that Taoist masters wrote songs and poems
on fallen leaves and then threw them
into fast-moving mountain streams, laughing.

Or they would scribble them with plum branches
on marble smooth ponds reflecting the distant stars,
only to have them explode brilliantly
by surprised old bullfrogs meditating there.

But the songs play on in my head. Sometimes,
it's just rush hour traffic buzzing there in the background.

But sad can get happy, too, like when it's Ray's big band,
backed-up by the Raelettes, of course, and everyone's playing
and singing like angels.

Sometimes though, it's Bud Powell's melancholy trio
or maybe just you at the baby grand in the lobby,
tinkling away at some silent *Chopsticks,* somewhere
East of the sun and West of the moon.

The Moth and the Flame

I, the moth, and you, the candle flame,
or me the flame and you the burning moth?

Or am I Chuang Tzu's butterfly dreaming
he is the burning sage? Or you the burning flame,
flaming for my dreaming moth?

Regardless of our current incandescent incarnations,
some magic draws us in to spin in our tiny orbits
about that hot flame tip, that moth wing,
that dreaming sage.

In the morning, so often during our day, on towards
tea-time and then into that violet hour, dusk,
our fleeting moments between day and night,

or 'round midnight, between sweet dreams
and our restless awakening,
between candle flame and love's ash—

(the now).

Chuang Tzu (c. 369 - c. 286 BCE) Poet, philosopher, landscape painter and significant interpreter of Taoism. He greatly influenced Chinese Buddhism and landscape painting. Chuang Tzu was to Lao-Tzu as Plato was to Socrates, as far as we know.

Discussing the Storm

We discuss the pending storm
and the time of its probable passing,
while sitting here on this quiet hilltop
looking through Winter's leafless trees
at the slow muddy river below.

No green yet, all earth, khaki
and white-tailed deer as we watch
the grey-blue clouds above hurry on their way.

The predicted storm blows through finally,
as expected, good and loud, a real harbinger
of patient Spring.

Ready or not, here it comes, that giant hail
smashin' down on my bitchin' ride.

Joining The Mermaids

The deafening soft susurrus of the cicadas
comes in my open window over the hum
of my neighbor's raucous air conditioner.

All seems calm. All seems well. Then suddenly,
out of nowhere, a huge branch falls from some
dying tree nearby with an incredible, electrifying *CRACK!*

A feral cat howls into the sweltering dawn.
I sullenly rise, shut the window, turn on my air
and sink back into the deep sea of sleep.

Mermaids beckon to me from just beyond the breakwater
and I swim on down with my pillow, to join them.

A Crack Only

While in the tub tonight, washing away my sins
on the new moon, I opened my tiny window,
a crack only.

Spring wetness rushed in, and you with it,
carried in on the wings of the church bells tolling
across the way.

It's not really all that far, just the distance
between my tears and the rain.

Leaving Poems on the Floor

I like leaving poems in my notebook, on the desk
or scattered on the floor by the bed.
In the dark, I write them down
and then close the book on them.

It gives me a lovely *frisson* to stumble across them later.
Sometimes I remember them, other times I forget.
They all flow together like rivulets
running into our one great sea.

But to leave them unfinished, laying around,
is such a subtle joy, a real thrill of so few.
I once found a bunch of them in the bottom of a basket,
under some files, long lost and forgotten.

They all turned out rather well, in the end, I think.
To find them, to turn them into something
other than archeology is a fine thing,
something to read to Ernest Hemingway
in a clean well-lighted place,
preferably in Cuba.

In The Old Neighborhood

When I returned here to the old neighborhood
I took to walking the trails through the woods and hills
of our park, just behind my old place

and occasionally, I would stumble across pieces
of broken pottery lying in my way, uncovered by
the simple archeology of the seasons.

Shards they are, little broken shards of lives gone by.
Little things, made and used by others, now broken,
cast aside in both time and space.

Just imagine, so long ago, a wet hand and dish towel,
an accidental slip, a clumsy, missed catch then
the tiny tragic fall of a quick-to-shatter teacup
or its saucer, now in little pieces for me to find,
in a century or so, somewhere along my path.

To the Blonde Tara

With no thought of recompense, whatsoever
your unbounded love for me shines forth
from your glowing generous heart.

I drive around town, weeping and laughing
simultaneously in the cool noon rain.
Oh yes, I'm happy and chilling,

though at times I wonder about the Muse,
and whether or not she requires further
demonstrable evidence of my angst.

Well, if that be the case, I'm sorry,
and fervently apologize.
Sacrifices certainly must be made.

People are beginning to turn and stare:
funny girls in coffee shop windows,
broken down bus loads of pilgrims
somewhere along their path.

Grumbling google-eyed dudes
in used bookstores recognize my shiny aura
and I slap them down, gently, with my smile.

Strange homeless Buddha's follow me in droves,
looking for a lift and a big nickel.
I happily relinquish both and speed on towards
your big Buddha heart.

It's time, it's time.

OM TARE TUTARE SVAHA

Tara – A Tibetan Buddhist Bodhisattva who comes in many colors—red, white, green, black, yellow and more. Early on she resolved to be reincarnated only as a female until *Samsara* is no more. She is a Buddha of enlightened activity, a savioress who embodies compassion, long life, healing, serenity, good fortune as well as the transmutation of anger.

These Leaves

It is not everyone that has your passion for dead leaves.
-Jane Austen

These leaves falling around my head:
orange, russet, amber, yellow and brown.

I crumble them noisily as I walk down my path,
making delicious food for the little ones
that will eat me when I, in turn,
turn blue and f
                a

        l

                l.

The Monkey Lab

There's still no word from the monkey lab, as I stroll
by your corner watching the night rise up around me.

I wouldn't have recognized it as prosaic as it is now,
this Summer's eve. It's not as it was then in that thunderous
rainy Spring.

But this night there happens to be a morbid hominid family
ensconced on your corner, looking at me incredulously
as I pass like maybe I don't really belong on their tattooed
planet of the apes.

Obviously, much research needs to be done on the
Homo sapien's brain and clan structure. We're not really
all that far uphill from our cousins so happy in their trees.

Now, as I stroll towards the edge of my raggedy map,
somewhere on this lost continent seeking dinner
and ice cream, I wonder:

Any word from the monkey lab?

There be monsters here.

Wireless Out Here

It's all wireless out here, on this desert trail through time.
I've travelled for days it seems, with nary a people person
in sight.

The stupid fences and lonesome telephone poles
are all that remain of man's unconscious thumbprint
on the land.

Ancient roads fade into nothingness, giant rocks
like dragon's teeth snarl up from the right-of-way,
towering over me as I toil uphill into the west wind.

In the distance, rounded hillocks rise and fall
like sweet breasts, pushing against the mighty
clouds hanging above the skyline, blue-grey
against the distant horizon.

Beyond that, rain falls. Maybe.

Slow Boats and Magic Mountains

Just seeing you again, the other day, your hair up,
way nonchalant, was like finding a missing piece
of my puzzle, lost down behind my armoire,
hidden there, just out of reach.

We're all just trying to live our lives,
creating ourselves anew from the dust and ashes
of our wildly checkered pasts.

There is so much bound-up energy and forward inertia
in them and we so unconsciously lay out our orbits
around this mad little asteroid.

Our gravities sometimes attract, sometimes repel.
The chances are somewhere between slim and none
that such skewed trajectories should ever cross again.

It's miraculous even, like living beyond our biblically
allotted four score and ten. Our time here grows short.

The days and nights flicker and blink back at us
like old movies. Space, time and matter
becomes muddled. Only love can clarify.
The path wide, the gate narrow.

Our mystery ship picks up speed. Magic mountains ahead.

Swept Away

My window opens a crack to the past
and the rains of remembering.
All wet, I enter.

This stuff pouring down now reminds me
of other downfalls I've soaked up during
my time in space.

The ferocious pounding on the roof
of the old brown boathouse, just uphill
from the cold slate-gray lake in the fog.

And another early Spring rain, after a long, brutal
Ohio Winter soaks purple buds barely breaking through
last Fall's fallen leaves. Out my high window,
the bare trees are just out of reach.

And our own Midwestern gully-washers, so sudden,
flash flooding the land, splashing on steaming sidewalks,
driving the night crawlers from their homesteads.

To the gutters with them!

Swept away, refugees all.

Out On The Land

Did you get out on the land during your time away?
Did you and your loyal dog stroll on down
through the woods by that crystal clear stream?

I hope you did and that the deer and the raven
were out in numbers, following you both along the trail,
all dreaming of days gone by,

those days, before the great land-bridge crossing,
when sparkling musical streams were everywhere,
overflowing with salmon swimming upstream to breed
and downstream to die.

Those silent days unheard in the forest primeval,
the endless golden eons before man
and his clever, cold contraptions, now sold
so capriciously along the roadside
that end their full, useless lives
in some wrecking yard of scrap, rusting in the rain,

where junk yard dogs black as night with eyes like stars
keep lookout as they howl and pace there,
behind the imagined security of chain link fences.

They're angry and trapped inside, or better yet, perhaps,
they've finally, happily escaped, and are now running free
and sometimes, maybe, they might just stop for a moment
or two, somewhere on the well-worn path
beside that stream and wonder:

Am I missing someone?

That's The Thing

That's the thing about mountains,
you can't get them at Walmart,
and there's no free parking.

You always start at the bottom.
But with a mountain there's at least
a ghost of a chance of reaching the summit.

It's all about the walking, taking those steps,
one at a time, again and again and again
until your job's done.

Some folks push boulders up to the top
and others slide up on silk.
Both are the same amount of work.

Make it easy on yourself. Take your prayer wheel
and your pocket knife. You better start early,
pack a nice lunch and be ready to stay late.

Maybe a lifetime or two.

No Trains

There are no trains up on those bluffs and no river either.
It's always quiet and the shit still runs downhill.

All the important decisions are made up there,
in the cold candelabra'd rooms of the big houses,
where there's always plenty of oak-aged bourbon on ice,
sweet vermouth and silk panties on the floor,
still warm from the flesh of the most recent occupant.

Down here at the bottom, we await our orders,
just outside the worn-out levee with the trains,
the freight and the bags by the tired brown river.

There's cotton and *darkies,* down here, too,
along with plenty of dirty blue collars
and chaffing hot *rednecks.*

We all await the committee, the big white boys
in the know, working out the details up in their
smoke filled rooms. They so often remind us
that all we do down here, really, is serve.

But remember, Commandante, up or down,
the little people have big dreams, too,
and you may not be in them.

Minor Napoleonia

Aidez-moi, ma chere amie.
　　　　　–Jean-Paul Marat

My collection of minor Napoleonia looks down upon me
from my walls and shelves, unlikely and improbable gifts
from my people.

The antique hand-tinted print of the little Emperor, at play,
en famille, in the palace garden of *Le Petite Trianon*
shows his arms outstretched as if to encompass the world,
his toy troops scattered disastrously at his feet,
his own future unseen.

My own troops, tiny Hussars or Grenadiers, I believe,
are locked away in their own dusty, cobwebbed armoire,
there on parade, confused, lost and fallen,
now only fighting giant spiders.

My *faux* golden inkwell is perhaps just some tourist relic,
shaped like the Emperor's tomb, twinkling back at me
from my busy desk, and like my life, is beautiful, empty,
surrounded by things so tarnished.

And later, I, like Marat, sink back into my own tub,
pen in hand, bleeding from losses incalculable
from my own skirmishes, candles guttering away
in my candelabra'd *maisonette.*

All revolution quelled, *pour le moment.*

The Miracle of Leverage

The best return on any investment I ever made
was splitting my daffodil bulbs this afternoon.
It was, finally, time for me to realize the fruition
of their hard work.

I slid my old garden spade under the masses
of buried bulbs and entire mounds broke free
from the dark underworld, beneath.

They came up in huge tranches, far exceeding
any expectations of profit or projected rate of return.
Oh! The miracles of leverage, compounding
and the slow patience required for long term growth!

I filled two pickle buckets, a paper bag, a tub
and an old cardboard box with the beautiful brown,
earthy bulbs.

I was so swept away by the enormity of the actual
realized return versus my small initial investment,
that I forgot a very, important, previously scheduled
engagement.

I need to be somewhere else, now. Right now!
Of course! I'll just go ahead and slide on over
like glaciation, cool and old, delivering both
bulbs and boulders.

On A Beautiful Day Like This

On a beautiful day like today who could not believe?
No more prisoners of love or any other crimes,
all executions stayed, pending yet another appeal.
All pets freed at last.

The stores are open all around the world
giving the people what they want and need.
The postman rings twice, drops his bag and runs,
laughing down our empty, silent street.

The hospital beds are empty today by checkout time.
TV's around the world are off.
There is always something more interesting
happening out in the street.

All the brokenhearted lovers awaken, energized,
feelin' the healin.' Maybe it really wasn't anyone's fault?

The big man forgives us all as he climbs down
from his tree and takes a hike,
looking for a tall cool drink,
a fallen woman and some Band-Aids.

Over in the 'hood, a foolhardy handyman
in his dark basement puts down his tool
and heads out into the backyard and says,

Yeah, man. Maybe I'll plant a tree!

Strange Magic Incarnate
for Randolph Getty

One day you and I will take that *camionetta*
or perhaps even a languid, silver Hindenburg
on down to *Inca-land,* to touch those ancient walls,

now eternally quiet and not unfriendly
in their own dark way. They are strong
and grounded enough to hold back the Andes forever.

Those stone walls, emissaries from another age,
are bound up in some strange magic incarnate
from that lost time, when giant stones were feathers
and wheel-less man, the mason.

Loud and Clear

It is the simple power of water that slowly drips,
drips, drips from my kitchen faucet, wearing down
that old sink, that grimy tub, my arteries
and those Grand Canyon walls. So what am I to that?
Surely just a small fry and a medium joke.

All and all it's just eternal quiet erosion,
endlessly working and wearing everything thin
as I head down stream towards my own final dissolution.

No shit, indeed. All that means nothing, to say, television.
All our fine words and beautiful pictures,
now sent out amongst the whirling galaxies,
eternally receiving us, loud and clear, or so they say.

But, please, try to keep that infernal noise down
as you stroll across your worn-out parking lot,
to then stumble, blindly, through that dark forest,
and slip, silently, back into the empty, warming sea.

I Live Alone Now

I live alone now, much to my chagrin and relief.
The blessings fall like morning dew on the poison ivy.

No one can tell me *bupkus* anymore
and there's not that much really that I have to do.

I'm looking forward to the Winter, cold as death
while someone else cuts the wood and stokes the fire.

There will be plenty of time then to sift through my papers,
in amongst the stacks of dog-eared books and oddments.

Plenty of cold quiet time then to rewrite every page
and file them away for Spring.

Rural Drama

Poison ivy grows thickly on one side of my broken stoop,
several gruesome thorny cacti on the other—
my own *Scylla* and *Charybdis*.

A huge thicket of thorny roses reaches out to cover the house,
blocking my door. The grass needs cutting desperately
and suckers are coming up everywhere.

A lonely Red Tailed Hawk flies directly overhead, stationary
in the afternoon breeze. Our tabby cat is hunting in the field
just outside the back door, always on the lookout
for birds and bunnies, relishing both.

My black coffee reflects the cloudless sky—
super Buddha-mind blue today, washed clean
by the mighty rains we've had all week up here,
way North of the river, far from the calamities of the city.

The people there leave me alone now, more or less.
Their drama seems only like distant bells whose echo
just doesn't seem to reach across the brown and flooded river.

Our rural drama here amounts to, at most, a wasp or a rooster
getting into the house and wandering about unescorted
or perhaps a possum family rustling about under the house.

The big tractor mows on, cutting only the widest swaths
of our acreage, as if to say, *Don't sweat the small stuff.*

I've big plans for those roses but they will wait, won't they?

Further comments have been filed with the Tibetan Embassy
down the road. We patiently await the Ambassador's laugh
and answering wave.

The *Ticks* of the *Tock*

There is a sameness to our days, all strung out
like tiny stars in our asteroid belt.

But there are not that many of them, are there,
numbered or unnumbered? No one knows
from instant to instant what is left, dregs or delight?
Our cups, half-empty, half-full or overflowing
into their lovely matching saucers?

Is there more fore or aft? Port or starboard?
It really doesn't matter much does it?
It's all now, right now, anyway.

We count our years, months, weeks, days, minutes,
the seconds, and now, the nano-seconds of modern
scientific time on semi-elegant timepieces, everywhere.

The *ticks* of the *tock,* bangs of the gong, the memos,
the mail, the quarter, the half, the season,
the fade, the draw, the putt, the chip, the drive,
the stumble, the fall, the beginning or the inning.

We personally dissect each one, trying to pluck
some sort of life from it, somehow, I suppose.

We get up, struggle into our outfits and hurry on down
into the traffic jam to do our time.

There's really not that much mirth in it, is there?
It seems forced, phony and tasteless,
the way we half-bake the days of our lives
instead of living them at a fast roiling boil.

We all work so hard at digging our ruts,
and we spend our lives so lovingly decorating them.
You get all comfortable and cozy down in that
hard drivin' groove and, well,

it's *groovy.*

Crickets in Fall

Crickets in Fall, timely brown leaves on my front step,
or anywhere else for that matter, shoes all akimbo
in dust under the bed, just out of reach, of course.

Too many books on shelves, disorganized by subject,
with untraveled maps hidden away with their distant
neighbors, cracks in window panes and out that same
grimy window, cracks in ancient up-heaved sidewalks,
and then, of course, breezes mussing your hair,
any season I see you in.

And later, more crickets, a different species, no doubt,
summer's wheelbarrow left out alone, languishing for months,
still filled with giant stones, Great Pyramids abandoned.

But closer at hand: pencils, paper, the poet's inspired product
in stacks on chairs—aggravating piles. Wrinkled sheets
(not paper), on an unmade bed of nails represents
long journeys, off somewhere, but here too, scribbling away,

having them spilled, in confused profusion,
across the great ocean floor of mind, where the sharks,
sea snakes, newly-discovered giant radioactive crabs,
benthic isopods and long sunken treasure-filled galleons
of metaphor await the exhausted explorer, grasping for breath,
drowning again.

Most Young Men

All comes to vanish, even the memory of the father in the son.
        -Adolphe Martial-Patémont

Most young men don't have time for poetry.
With them, it's all go, go, go, the next girl,
the next bomb.

But they'll find out, won't they
(those who make it, that is),
that poetry is an old man's game.

He's someone who has no precious time to spare,
who throws away hours and hours,
fussing with piles of paper, making notes.

He's scratching on scraps, looking for pens,
pencils and paper in the dark, wondering
where it comes from and where it all goes,

while the young man is out dancing in the loud
(or should be) and the old man is home,
shrinking and growing all the while,
waiting for the young man to catch up,
knowing really, that he can't and never will.

the seconds

the seconds are tiny and there are so many of them

they fit together perfectly like the black and white keys
on accordions but make nary a sound,
somehow just barely holding it all together

the laugh track will be added later in a dreary office
somewhere down the hall

the clicking of the soundless seconds grows to fill a life
as that laugh reel rolls on, amusing the children

the wheel of the clocks *tick tocks* each day,
every instant the same and different, too
on Earth as on Mars—

it's warmer here and the wind blows just the same

An Anarchist Miracle

We slough off ourselves, unconsciously scattering
dead skin and microbial life in invisible clouds
everywhere we go.

Our little engines rev-up, for better or worse,
pretty much captain-less, an anarchist miracle
that seems to work remarkably well.

These little engines are inevitably powered
by the sun, our old Uncle Sol, if you will,
a loving and benign relative on one hand,
but also brutal and unforgiving if one steps
too far out of the shade.

One's control should remain oblique,
the engine idling, calm and aware, lots of pure water,
great fuel, immense love and sweet dreams, kiddo.
Too much of anything just doesn't work long term.

Our spatial auras extend beyond this heirloom flesh
upwards of sixty feet (or so they say at Science City),
a possible energetic, if not occasionally, visual proof
that the engines are turning over nicely,
thank you very much.

Auras radiate out from our *chakras,* touching all we pass,
like that homeless fella on the corner there,
sitting in a patch of dappled morning sun,
bathed in his own auric field, no doubt, fueled by gin.

A Poem, Hopefully Countering Your Disbelief in Reincarnation

Who has not walked in the woods,
down a country lane or along a beach
and spied a fallen leaf, a stone,
hickory nut, or this seashell?

Perhaps it was once a home to someone,
but it's now vacant and pounded smooth
by the ancient sea, just waiting there,
to be recognized by another someone
from somewhere,

to be picked up and casually slipped
into a pocket or reticule, carried
for miles and miles, then pressed,
gently, into another warm, loving hand.

Here, it's you, I remembered.

We Never Auditioned

We never auditioned for our parts in this little human play.
You, the nameless heroine and me, the fallen hero,
returning to you without my shield.

The years have been kind to us, regardless of our excuses.
Our needs are simple, really. But it's not easy, after all,
to cast off the dross.

There's always the perpetual refinement problem, isn't there,
that ubiquitous upgrade coefficient.

I mean, really, a lap pool for our tears to swim in.

Every Man Dreaming of Crime

*The one true Surrealist act is to step down into the street
with guns blazing into the awaiting crowd.*
–Pierre Reverdy

Please, don't bother with a Quick Trip or 7-11!
Go ahead, shoot for the big time like the New York Fed
or Bank of America where the dollars are always laying about,
shrink-wrapped, neatly stacked, dry cleaned
and freshly laundered, patiently waiting on pallets in the dark.

Even better would be an armored car job, working outside,
being the get-away driver or the mastermind, snatching up
all that cold, hard cash in small, dirty unmarked bills,
stashed in big duffel bags down in your crawl-space.

Peeling off a couple of hundreds every morning
could certainly help with expenses. You could become
a lifestyle consultant or financial adviser.

But please, don't hurt anyone and remember *Surrealism*
always raises its beautiful head whether you're ready or not.

It's in all the movies.

At Three Gorges with Li Po

As I open a long lost book of Li Po,
your face appears as a *Kwan Yin*
on the frontispiece.

My throat, heart and solar plexus open,
deep as the Three Gorges: Li Po, you—
and me, working for *kalpas*
just to pour your wine.

Kwan Yin - the Buddhist goddess embodiment of compassion and loving kindness

Kalpa - 4.32 billion years in Buddhist cosmology or the amount of time for Mt. Everest to completely wear away when the mythical Garuda bird flies over its summit once every 100 years, brushing the peak with a sacred silk scarf.

One Breath

We use up this world
one breath
one kiss
one bite at a time.

We use up this world
like there is no tomorrow
one sip
one big gulp
one tankful at a time—

hungry little animals running scared.

Twin Bed

I just got this twin bed.
It's just about big enough for me
and a tiny Pekingese.

My non-heirloom china
is broken and cracked,
none of it matches.
*There is no spoon.**

My only friends are sardines,
lying dead, packed straight and tight
in their tiny tins. I eat them
with dry, speechless crackers.

I hate to confess, I mostly sleep
on my left side which
is bad for the heart.

But, what isn't?

*The Matrix, 1999

Here Again

Today is here again,
up so bright and early
or so it seems.
The hands of the clock—
clang, clang, clang, into my dreams.

A sad river flows by
under the willows on the shore
washing the rocks as it goes.

A hell of a job, if you ask me.
The light hits the surface just right
but that's as deep as it gets.

The Princess and the Peacock

It's really pretty cool to think of our own limits,
those tiny circles that we draw around our lives,
our dreams, our energy.

Oh well, you might rationalize, that's not really for me.
I'm a poet, one truly grounded in that pure ephemeral light.
The only search engine I need is a thesaurus.

Perhaps you only want to help, to sacrifice yourself
on the altar of others. Or you draw that tiny circle
around your life with bottles, candles or rope.

But think of the very rich and their pathetic lives,
the expensive bad taste, the endless striving
for perfection, ever receding into that eternal mirage,

always awaiting good help, finally,
or for the Princess to call
and the peacocks in the garden, always messing.

And then Fall comes, dropping leaves everywhere.

Darn That Dream!

Oh yeah, poetry school. Sure, I need more class:
how to find a fucking pencil-stub in the dark,
how to write in bed without getting carpal tunnel neck,
how to memorize whole insipid poems while asleep,
eliminating the middlemen in all fifty dream states.

Remember those effervescent verses? My eyelid twitches,
the malarial night sweats and the restless legs,
wandering where and kicking whom or what?

Darn that dream! Where's that notebook?
It's here somewhere, back under that armoire again,
I'm sure.

Wait, wait. I hear birds.

The Great Peregrination

I miss the snow geese stopping off here in Spring.
They've gone on North looking for better food
and cleaner water, I guess.

To see a gaggle fly overhead, in a perfect V-formation,
is truly joyous. Sometimes it's just two, mated for life, they say.

It sure looks good, flying around pair-bonded
like that. Truly, until death do they part.

No lawyers, no *prenupts,* just pure agreement,
wordless consensus, day in, day out,
such a seamless expression of wonder.

We should be so lucky—no words,
just honking at each other every day,
flying into the bright, cloud-filled sky,
South for the winter.

Mexico, hon? Florida's burning!

1998 - A year of great fires in Florida's Okefenokee Swamp

Dawn Breaks

Dawn breaks hard here on the Great Plains.
The road rises to meet the clouds strung out
across our morning sky—

three grey-white stragglers,
like giant misplaced punctuation:
a comma and a semi-colon.

My own tiny steam cloud rises from a coffee cup
balanced precariously on the dash,
obscuring the windshield, the highway
and the future, dead ahead.

A gaggle of snow geese takes their coffee break
in a flooded brown field.

A Bird's Careful Life

If indeed there be rewards for those acts,
those pure, selfless, heroic acts, the good acts,
performed above and beyond the requirements
of daily banal existence, then one of those
possible rewards might be one's reincarnation
as a bird.

To return to earth, hatched from a warm egg,
born again, a descendant of dinosaurs, far and away
the most wonderful earthbound family
to belong to, even if so distantly.

Then there is the flying, so lavish and nonchalant,
anywhere, anytime, an experience so seamless
and unfathomable to us earthly admirers, trapped here
by our dear friend and implacable enemy, gravity.

Even more surrealistically improbable would be
the Zen-like sitting, so gently, on one's own eggs,
alone for long periods, in a nest, fed by significant others,
creating noisy, hungry life from perfect shells.

Our bird lives large, no more brushing of teeth
but rather just daintily washing up in dewdrops
and pristine puddles somewhere, carefully out of the way
of windows and windmills.

Fine Horseflesh

I was in the tub this marvelous afternoon
reading your *Nine Horses,* from back to front this time,
when suddenly I realized that we had a lot more
in common than just fine horseflesh and the Laureate,

yours, nobly past (all now stand in your considerable shadow)
and mine—somewhere on a long, strange and skewed orbit
towards a galaxy light years away, in another life,
and as you know, in the poetic universe, time and space
don't matter.

But we do share a fine friendship, too,
beyond the fickle, fickle muse. Our mutual friend
met you here and she had you for dinner.

You were lovely, she said.

Nine Horses, Poems by Billie Collins

Our National Pastime

I never much liked guys in uniforms,
their stinking gyms, the smelly cold concrete,
the incessant spitting and towel snapping
in frigid locker rooms.

In my youth, I was seldom part of a team.
I usually played alone, unable to comprehend
the timeless, open-ended rules of the game
or the elegant, gentlemanly nature of play.

I was unable, then, to take the long view of my short stop,
here, and I had not yet felt the victorious primal power
of the home run.

But I sit here now, on the front porch,
in my old rocking chair, weeping to see
the Angels getting trounced by the Devils, again.

So Sorry, Old Chap
for Jason Ryberg

Sorry, so sorry, old chap, to miss the poets reading, again,
but that time of day, I tend to blink and wither
at the thought of approaching dusk.

I fade off into unconscious napdom, powerless to recover
from an exhausting lifetime of opinions and wordless dreams.

You all read on. I hear your mutterings from afar
as the surf of sleep crashes over my pillow. Silent songbirds
peek in my window again, curious still.

Jung and Freud appear in dreamland, still fighting:
nature or nurture, cigars or cocaine, archetypes or neurosis,
with me stretched out on the couch between them,
oblivious in oblivion.

A sweet dreaming prince, so innocent, so vulnerable,
all stress, all imagination gone, as my tub fills slowly
from the drain b
              e
           l
              o
                 w.

SPDRS and ZEBRAS

It really is quite mystical. The market, I mean.
It's more than the opening gavel or the final bell.
It's the ancient tape, the obsessive charts
and that big fat ball of intuitive fear in the belly,
hiding under those rock hard abs.

The boys on the trading floor in their funny jackets
and suspenders are ceaselessly cranking out the trades,
unconsciously comodifying the digestive processes
of our species' conversion of one form of energy
into another.

The middle men, eternally in the way,
elbow the little guy back from the trough
with their silver spoons and sand wedges.

Some day though, our savings being compounded
as generously as they are, we'll all be knee-deep
in our own debentures, warrants and indictments,
shorting our *ZEBRAS* from long positions deep inside
our *SPDR* holes.

How can this not be entropic nature at work?
Yeah, all the sectors, all the time.

SPDRS: a family of exchange traded funds. ZEBRAS: an interest rate swap between a municipality and a financial institution.

Another Bud

Another bud has stumbled and fallen
in this walk through the park.

The line behind him is neither longer nor shorter.

We all shuffle in place until our moment arrives.

It is all now—past, present, future, history.

Make the best of it.

He did.

A Word to the Wise Guy
for William Seward Burroughs

In my dream, I walked by your open casket
and there you were, in your dark suit, hands on your hat,
your ritual tools all laid out for that lonely trip
across the River Styx into a *Bardo* all your own.

The cane and bullwhip, the trusty typewriter,
that wreath of *yagé,* a thick pad of scripts
signed by some croaker and, of course,
your favorite handgun—a real man stopper,
(not some little lady's gun).

They're all laid out in your funeral barge, ready now
for that last, long voyage down to the black vastness
of the *Upper Baboon Asshole.*

Whither thou goest, may you find that silence,
that final extermination of the virus language
you long searched for.

And so, what is your legacy? Billions terminally infected
but millions more now looking beyond the flimsy tissue
of culture and mind into the eyes of the true self
and the moment:

no god, no mother, no flag.

That Final Cool Somewhere
for Jack Kerouac

I've been thinking about Jack and his apocryphal manuscript, a hundred twenty feet long, in a roll and on a roll, taped and glued, scratched and typed, folded and molded, spewing forth his words, his glory story, endless, seamless and fragile like life, punctuated with his loves, deaths, breaths and doors, opening and closing in old cars and trucks, not his, of course, but somehow ours, ever ready to roll, stolen, loaded and just flyin' out that open door, fresh, right off the floor into that perfect sky blue astral overdrive, always ready to roll endlessly across the Great Plains of theirs. No, it certainly ain't ours and it won't ever be ours, this land, but maybe we can get out there to that final cool somewhere on their super slab, driving and riding their cars, trucks and trains, stolen and loaded, trunks and backseats, cattle cars and coal, overflowing with the world's abundance brought to you alone through the magic of advertising, cheap oil, global crime, big time murder and shopping. Everything you ever dreamed of is nothing but suffering, the sad shimmering mirage of Hollywood's Buffet America, that ravenous 24-hour ghost stuttering and staggering along the ramparts of the world, always hungry, always empty, drivin' into smoke, signifying nothing,
Jack.

When My Time

When my time finally flickers and fades at *last call*,
they'll have to pull the bad pictures and tiny poems
off this tired old brain exhausted by so many years
of, well, just livin' the dream,

breathing deep the black smoke of internal combustion
and exhaling the fragrance of daffodils
into each brand new baby day.

Down at Science City, they'll upload the stories,
both sad and glad, as well as all the little unscripted
cinematic clips of days gone by that rest here,
filed away just behind my eyes.

They better hurry.

A Treatise in a Smile
for Gregory Sherman Pierson

Remember when we were young
and the world was our oyster,
when every car was a speedster
and every girl had her top down?

The music was sweeter and the wine
more full-bodied then. Our friends
were beautiful and lived forever.

Not so lately. These days it's all the rage
and me now dizzy with vertigo
as another bud stumbles and falls.
He did his duty and served us well.

Will we live to regret this? I expect so.
We enter for free but pay with our lives.
Our time here is brief like a spark across a gap.

Moments to go, seconds to live,
our life is our monument,
a treatise in a look, volumes in a smile.

The Poem's Cooked
for Louise

These poems are never finished, never complete.
They bloom in the Fall and drop their fruit in the Spring.
They lie, soaked and gasping, just outside the levee,
having miraculously escaped the great flood.

When nearly ripe, I pluck them from their branches,
carry them gently into the kitchen to set them
on the window sill in the sun.

Finally, I pick the one and bite down hard
to get at its sweet, nutty goodness.

May Already

Oh Lord, is it May already?

The clocks tick ever faster. No. They tick the same,
inexorably, like saving daylight, our instants
saved up and stored for later.

Yeah, that clock, steady as my shallow restless pulse.

The days pass like clouds crossing the sky, always beautiful.
My thoughts and dreams are never real and they too pass
like the clouds.

I wake. I walk. I sleep. I dream my way
through these cinematic days and nights.

Jesus, you mean, it's November?

what is called a hill

I live on top of what is called a hill around here,
above a reasonably busy street just North of town

the people in their cars and trucks speed by,
to and fro, up and down my hill, always busy,
always racing–rarin' to go somewhere else,
certainly more important than here

but there are remarkably, times and spaces
when it is totally silent in all directions,
no wind through the trees, no cars, nothing nowhere

that's what wakes me, the total loudness
of the silence–no birds, no cars, no breeze,
no ambulances chasin' back up the hill
to the bone yard

I count that time, not by numbers as such
but by the cadence of moments
between the soft sibilant whoosh
of car tires on warm asphalt,

between the walls of silence on either end,
of those moments, down there
where the rubber meets the road

nothing now, only the waiting for the next one to pass–
moment, vehicle, emptiness to be filled

Ah, yes! there goes another one

After Dinner Remarks

So let us now take this time to mark our accomplishments.
We have achieved our majority plus some years,
in one piece, our beauty intact,
and our livers functioning, modestly, at least.

Most have obtained a modicum of shelter,
albeit the requisite sloughing off of dead
and deteriorating integument.

Several of us have significantly pair-bonded,
much to their credit or stupidity. Others have made
valiant attempts and so far have temporarily failed,
even with extensive assistance but, alas, without
full final fruition. No fault, no blame.

Some have off-sprung as is required
by the genetic imperative, biological metaphor,
evolution, and our own particular gonadal wind.

We have buried, burned, and otherwise faced up to
the endings of others and inevitably our own,
the former reminding us so painfully of the latter.

Some have claimed their patrimony or matrimony,
what there was of it. In many cases there turned out
to be far more than was ever fully accounted for
originally and mostly we have earned every penny.

What we do now is our business, no matter what our heirs and heiresses may think. The torch and shovel will be passed to them soon enough, as will their cross, millstone and albatross.

A Father's Job, That

Here Phaeton lies who in the sun-god's chariot fared.
And though greatly he failed, more greatly he dared.
                                        –Edith Hamilton

Icarus fell from the big blue sky one day
but not from a lack of trying.
A pair of finely crafted wings, handmade
by his genius father, of course, were

created to help him escape from the infamous
labyrinth, so often seen in old movies
and paintings, leaving the family Minotaur behind.

We don't know and can't ever know Icarus
or his father's plan for him, unless, of course,
we ourselves set our own plans in motion, taking off,
riding up into the gleaming sun, like Phaeton,

that other rich kid with a great tan, wanting so badly
to borrow that cool golden chariot out in the drive.
He's dying to race daddy's giant horses, can't wait
to chase all those girls across the morning sky,
but then he'll lose, big time, setting our world on fire.

You, too, might imagine or remember, the clouds parting,
the blinding sun at its merry zenith, the wax burning hot
on strong young arms as it melts and drips
and then the cry of sudden surprise
when the brakes don't work.

But that's life, ain't it? Unstoppable except at the end.

bask in the light

the moon is up, the sun is down

the yawping frogs bask in the light
of the distant stars, twinkling

like freshly polished silver
on the sideboard
at a banquet of knaves

the frogs clamoring at that moon
as it wheels across our big, empty sky

cicadas sing their praises

The Voices, All Mine

I shut the door behind me.
My world opens wide
and the silence begins.

The music of my aloneness,
the voices, all mine—singing,
chatting, sometimes cursing,
sometimes screaming.
My clenched fists, my smiles,
my endless tears of joy and rage.

The doors all open inward
into the narrow hallway of my gallery,
all my victims are there,
all my children, all my muses,
and portraits of all my ghosts.

I wander around in circles,
sleep in many beds for many rooms
has my mini-mansion.
Many breaths have I breathed here,
many a sigh of relief and regret.

My Plaster Sky

We have often walked, the two of us,
in the woods above the slow, brown river.

And now, after just such a walk, I lay here in my
darkened room and notice a thin shaft of yellow light
forcing itself in upon me through a tiny crack
in my moth-eaten drapes.

It falls, by chance, upon a lighted wall switch
and the pair joins there briefly to become a small comet
that pauses momentarily on my bedroom's plaster sky,
never to crash somewhere near my closet door.

That yellow light passes from form to form, ending up
here in my bedroom on this small scrap of paper,
after passing through the vastness of space, our world,
a streetlight, a cracked window pane, my pen, and me.

So we walk on, you and I, not even holding hands,
into that red, red sunset, the father of us all.

the laughing musical stream of life

                                          just keeps on splashing

    laughing along with every little drop

every tiny flood

        every sodden tear

                they cascade

                            on down

all around

                and over every instant

          every tiny jot and tittle is wet

   with the moments

        yours alone   or so you think

they all connect so perfectly   so congruently

      smooth as silk   so seamlessly

that it just can't be imagined going down any other way

the rivulets, the springs, the falls

    the big ones way out there on the horizon

     even the tiny wet seeps everywhere

even on the dryest days
     the gutters full of life and
leaves just spill over
   washing every second

happily, tragically or magically
     any which way
       but you say how
  just watch out

     you could be

(surely as the monsoons come)

sucked under hard

     eaten by whales

       if you're not careful

if you can't swim or float or surf or paddle a bit

   the rip-tides can get ya
      pull you under

   make you frown
 but you

                    the master plumber of
your life

                        always on call

                                  always there to fix it

                right then

            just try to relax

              if you hang loose or hang ten

even better
            then it's a gas

            and not just water splashing down on

                                        you

Cicadas Interrupted

the rainstorm begins slowly, sprinkling droplets
gently from clouds towering behind my trees

thunder builds in the distance, silencing the cicadas
in the grass

storm clouds can be clearly seen from every window,
out there, just over the silver barn on the hill

these dusty windows are covered with vines
some have broken into the house between the glass panes
and the old wood frames seeking any possible way in,

perhaps, a reminder to us all to persevere, somehow

church bells across the way annunciate the slow passage
of summer—one bell at the quarter hour,
two bells at the half, then three bells and whatever, straight up

cars race by—their sound, so far away in the distance,
is only a whoosh of white noise, just like the real world

thunder above the clouds rattles and booms,
shaking my dishes in their rack

big and little lightning flashes tease us—pink, red, gold
from behind the mountainous wall of grey clouds
rolling this way

darkness finally falls with the rain, now heavy
as it soaks every little thing,

a pair of red and black butterflies, casually seeking
sanctuary in my house, fly in through the open door,

and, of course, they immediately discover the half-closed,
vine-covered window and are trapped there,

throwing themselves furiously against the dirty glass,
time and time again, wanting only to escape
their new found refuge

then right on cue, an ambulance races up our hill,
mercifully, speeding on its way, coming to help, I assume

the rain finally stops and the cicadas pick up
where they left off, having barely missed a beat.

This Yeller Light

There is this yeller light that comes down around here
from outta the West, just before the big storms blow through.

The wind rustles the leaves, madly, like cowboys
on the Great Plains. The trees bend down
to bless the ground that birthed 'em.

Ah, but that yeller light, it comes through the clouds
hurrying by overhead. It sometimes seems almost orange
as the thunder echos across the hollow valley of the sky.

I hear that train in the distance honking, again and again,
telling me there's no way out of this one, ever—
no matter what.

I've found myself stumbling in this pouring damn heat
and I wonder if I too shouldn't just lay this old pillar
of salt and dust on down, to join Mama again.

Then finally the rain comes, dripping mightily
from the eaves onto my dear old daffodils,
now burnt up by that hot yeller light.

It fries the stuff that's weak, feeds the stuff that's strong
and gets us all in the end.

www.ingramcontent.com/pod-product-compliance
Lightning Source LLC
Chambersburg PA
CBHW021445080526
44588CB00009B/692